EASY PANINI
COOKBOOK

THE EFFORTLESS CHEF SERIES

VOL. #XXIX

By
Chef Maggie Chow
Copyright © 2015 by Saxonberg
Associates

Published by
BookSumo, a division of Saxonberg
Associates
http://www.booksumo.com/

A GIFT FROM ME TO YOU...

Send the Book!

I know you like easy cooking. But what about Japanese Sushi?

Join my private reader's club and get a copy of *__Infinite Sushi: A Complete Set of Sushi and Japanese Recipes__* by fellow BookSumo author Hashimoto Kazuma for FREE!

Send the Book!

Enjoy some of the best sushi available!

You will also receive updates about all my new books when they are free. So please show your support.

Also don't forget to like and subscribe on the social networks. I love meeting my readers. Links to all my profiles are below so please click and connect :)

Facebook

Twitter

ABOUT THE AUTHOR.

Maggie Chow is the author and creator of your favorite *Easy Cookbooks* and *The Effortless Chef Series*. Maggie is a lover of all things related to food. Maggie loves nothing more than finding new recipes, trying them out, and then making them her own, by adding or removing ingredients, tweaking cooking times, and anything to make the recipe not only taste better, but be easier to cook!

For a complete listing of all my books please see my author page.

INTRODUCTION

Welcome to *The Effortless Chef Series*!
Thank you for taking the time to
download the *Easy Panini Cookbook*.
Come take a journey with me into the
delights of easy cooking. The point of
this cookbook and all my cookbooks is to
exemplify the effortless nature of
cooking simply.

In this book we focus on Panini. You will
find that even though the recipes are
simple, the taste of the dishes is quite
amazing.

So will you join me in an adventure of
simple cooking? If the answer is yes
(and I hope it is) please consult the table
of contents to find the dishes you are
most interested in. Once you are ready
jump right in and start cooking.

— Chef Maggie Chow

TABLE OF CONTENTS

ANY ISSUES? CONTACT ME

If you find that something important to you is missing from this book please contact me at maggie@booksumo.com.

I will try my best to re-publish a revised copy taking your feedback into consideration and let you know when the book has been revised with you in mind.

:)

— Chef Maggie Chow

NOTICE TO PRINT READERS:

Hey, because you purchased the print version of this book you are entitled to its original digital version for free by Amazon.

So when you have the time, please review your purchases, and download the Kindle version of this book.

You might enjoy consuming this book more in its original digital format.

;)

But, in any case, take care and enjoy reading in whatever format you choose!

LEGAL NOTES

COMMON ABBREVIATIONS

cup(s)	C.
tablespoon	tbsp
teaspoon	tsp
ounce	oz
pound	lb

CHAPTER 1: EASY PANINI RECIPES

MOZZARELLA, TOMATO, BASIL

Ingredients

- 1 French deli roll, split
- 1 tsp balsamic vinegar
- 2 slices mozzarella cheese
- 1 small tomato, sliced
- 4 fresh basil leaves
- olive oil

Directions

- Heat up your skillet over medium heat.
- Spread some balsamic vinegar on a roll before putting mozzarella cheese, basil leaves, tomato slice

and the remaining cheese on top
of all this.
- Rub the outside with olive before
heating it up on the skillet for
about three minutes each side or
until you see that it golden brown
from the outside.
- Serve.

Serving: 1

Timing Information:

Preparation	Cooking	Total Time
10 mins	5 mins	15 mins

Nutritional Information:

Calories	402 kcal
Carbohydrates	29.9 g
Cholesterol	36 mg
Fat	24.1 g
Fiber	2.1 g
Protein	18.5 g
Sodium	613 mg

* Percent Daily Values are based on a 2,000 calorie diet.

TURKEY, SUNDRIED TOMATO, BASIL

Ingredients

- 4 Dinner Rolls, split
- Plain or sundried tomato mayonnaise (see below)
- 4 slices roast turkey or ham
- 4 slices Swiss, Monterey Jack, or Gruyere cheese
- 8 small slices red onion
- 1 C. fresh spinach leaves or several fresh basil leaves(optional)
- Salt and freshly ground black pepper
- Butter

Tomato Mayo:

- 1/4 C. mayonnaise
- 2 finely chopped sundried tomatoes

- Salt and freshly ground black pepper

Directions

- Spread mayonnaise and place all the ingredients except over roll.
- Grill sandwich on the Panini machine for seven minutes (three minutes if you are using a pan) after spreading some butter on the top and bottom.
- Whisk all the ingredients for mayonnaise together and set it aside for later use.

Serving: 4

Timing Information:

Preparation	Cooking	Total Time
10 mins	10 mins	20 mins

Nutritional Information:

Calories	464 kcal
Carbohydrates	40.8 g
Cholesterol	60 mg
Fat	26.6 g
Fiber	3.8 g
Protein	17.4 g
Sodium	936 mg

* Percent Daily Values are based on a 2,000 calorie diet.
☐

HUMMUS, EGGPLANT, MOZZARELLA

Ingredients

- 1 baby eggplant, cut into 1/4-inch slices
- salt and ground black pepper to taste
- 1/4 C. olive oil, divided
- 1 loaf flat bread, sliced horizontally and cut into 4 equal pieces
- 1/2 (12 oz) jar roasted red bell peppers, drained and sliced
- 4 oz shredded mozzarella cheese
- 1/4 C. roasted garlic hummus

Directions

- Coat eggplant slices with salt and pepper before letting it stand as it is for two minutes.

- Cook eggplant in batches in hot olive oil for about three minutes each side.
- Put eggplant, mozzarella cheese and red pepper over bread before spreading some hummus over the top piece of bread.
- Now grill these Paninis on a preheated Panini press for about 7 minutes or until the cheese has melted.

Serving: 1

Timing Information:

Preparation	Cooking	Total Time
15 mins	15 mins	30 mins

Nutritional Information:

Calories	401 kcal
Carbohydrates	41.5 g
Cholesterol	18 mg
Fat	21.7 g
Fiber	5.2 g
Protein	15.7 g
Sodium	625 mg

* Percent Daily Values are based on a 2,000 calorie diet.
□

CHICKEN, MONTEREY, BASIL PESTO

Ingredients

- 1 focaccia bread, quartered
- 1/2 C. prepared basil pesto
- 1 C. diced cooked chicken
- 1/2 C. diced green bell pepper
- 1/4 C. diced red onion
- 1 C. shredded Monterey Jack cheese

Directions

- Heat up your Panini grill according to the instruction of the manufacturer.
- Spread pesto over each half of focaccia bread before putting chicken, cheese, bell pepper and onion over the lower half, and closing it up to make a sandwich.

- Cook this Panini in the preheated grill for about 5 minutes or until the outside is golden brown.

Serving: 4

Timing Information:

Preparation	Cooking	Total Time
15 mins	5 mins	20 mins

Nutritional Information:

Calories	641 kcal
Carbohydrates	60.9 g
Cholesterol	61 mg
Fat	29.4 g
Fiber	4.4 g
Protein	32.4 g
Sodium	1076 mg

* Percent Daily Values are based on a 2,000 calorie diet.
☐

CHEDDAR, CHIPOTLE, CAESAR, BACON

Ingredients

- 2 slices sourdough bread
- 1/4 C. Caesar salad dressing
- 1 cooked chicken breast, diced
- 1/2 C. shredded Cheddar cheese
- 1 tbsp bacon bits
- 1 1/2 tsps chipotle chili powder, or to taste
- 2 tbsps softened butter

Directions

- Heat up your Panini grill according to the instruction of the manufacturer.
- Spread Caesar dressing over each half of the bread before putting chicken, cheddar cheese, bacon bits and chipotle chili powder

over the lower half, and closing it up to make a sandwich.

- Put some butter on top and cook this Panini in the preheated grill for about 4 minutes or until the outside is golden brown.

Serving: 1

Timing Information:

Preparation	Cooking	Total Time
10 mins	5 mins	15 mins

Nutritional Information:

Calories	1243 kcal
Carbohydrates	31.9 g
Cholesterol	312 mg
Fat	83.9 g
Fiber	1.5 g
Protein	85.7 g
Sodium	1813 mg

* Percent Daily Values are based on a 2,000 calorie diet.

☐

Romano, Basil, Chicken, Caesar

Ingredients

- 1/4 C. packed fresh basil leaves
- 1/4 C. olive oil
- 4 cloves garlic, diced
- 2 tbsps grated Romano cheese
- 1 tsp dried oregano
- 1 tsp ground black pepper
- 2 skinless, boneless chicken breast halves
- 2 tbsps creamy Caesar salad dressing
- 6 slices Italian bread with sesame seeds (Scali)
- 1/2 C. shredded iceberg lettuce
- 2 thin slices smoked mozzarella

Directions

- Heat up your grill and put some oil on the grate

- Blend a mixture of basil, oregano, oil, garlic, Romano cheese and pepper in a blender until smooth.
- Now grill chicken on the preheated grill for about 5 minutes each side.
- Spread Caesar dressing over the bread and put lettuce before putting additional slice of bread over it.
- Now put cooked chicken breast and smoked mozzarella before closing it up to make a sandwich.
- Cook this Panini in the preheated grill for about three minutes or until the outside is golden brown.

Serving: 2

Timing Information:

Preparation	Cooking	Total Time
20 mins	16 mins	36 mins

Nutritional Information:

Calories	587 kcal
Carbohydrates	20 g
Cholesterol	85 mg
Fat	41.5 g
Fiber	1.8 g
Protein	32.5 g
Sodium	523 mg

* Percent Daily Values are based on a 2,000 calorie diet.

☐

SOURDOUGH, PROVOLONE, PESTO

Ingredients

- 1/2 C. Extra Virgin Olive Oil
- 8 slices sourdough bread
- 1/4 C. pesto
- 16 thin slices Provolone cheese
- 12 thin slices prosciutto
- 4 whole, roasted red peppers, julienned

Directions

- Heat up your Panini grill according to the instruction of the manufacturer.
- Spread pesto over each half of the bread before putting ½ of cheese, prosciutto, pepper strips and the remaining cheese over the lower half, and closing it up to make a sandwich.

- Put some butter on top and cook this Panini in the preheated grill for about 4 minutes or until the outside is golden brown.

Serving: 4

Timing Information:

Preparation	Cooking	Total Time
15 mins	4 mins	19 mins

Nutritional Information:

Calories	798 kcal
Carbohydrates	27.4 g
Cholesterol	76 mg
Fat	63.9 g
Fiber	2.1 g
Protein	31 g
Sodium	1754 mg

* Percent Daily Values are based on a 2,000 calorie diet.
☐

AVOCADO, TURKEY, SPINACH, CIABATTA

Ingredients

- 4 slices artisan bread such as ciabatta
- 2 tsps honey Dijon salad dressing
- 1/2 C. baby spinach leaves
- 1/4 lb sliced oven-roasted deli turkey breast
- 1/4 red onion, cut into strips
- 1 ripe avocado from Mexico, peeled, pitted and thickly sliced
- Salt and pepper to taste
- 1/4 C. crumbled soft goat cheese
- Non-stick cooking spray

Directions

- Heat up your Panini grill according to the instruction of the manufacturer.

- Spread honey Dijon dressing, spinach leaves, turkey breast and red onion over lower half of the bread before putting avocado slices, salt, pepper and goat cheese over the upper half, and closing it up to make a sandwich.
- Put some butter on top and cook this Panini in the preheated grill for about 8 minutes or until the outside is golden brown.

Serving: 2

Timing Information:

Preparation	Cooking	Total Time
10 mins	10 mins	20 mins

Nutritional Information:

Calories	469 kcal
Carbohydrates	45.5 g
Cholesterol	37 mg
Fat	23.8 g
Fiber	8.5 g
Protein	22.1 g
Sodium	1250 mg

* Percent Daily Values are based on a 2,000 calorie diet.

MUSHROOM, SALAMI, HAM, PROVOLONE

Ingredients

- 1 tsp butter
- 2 tbsps sliced fresh mushrooms
- 1/2 C. tomato sauce
- 4 ciabatta rolls, split
- 2 cloves garlic, diced
- 1 tbsp dried oregano
- 8 slices hot Genoa salami
- 8 slices roasted ham
- 2 tbsps diced red onion
- 2 tbsps chopped roasted red pepper
- 2 tbsps chopped black olives
- 4 leaves basil, chopped
- 4 slices provolone cheese

Directions

- Heat up your Panini grill according to the instruction of the manufacturer.
- Cook mushrooms in hot butter for about seven minutes.
- Spread tomato sauce, garlic, oregano, salami slices, two slices of ham, red onion, basil, mushrooms, olives, red pepper and put provolone cheese in the very end over the lower half of the bread before closing it up to make a sandwich.
- Cook this Panini in the preheated grill for about 5 minutes or until the outside is golden brown.

Serving: 4

Timing Information:

Preparation	Cooking	Total Time
20 mins	5 mins	25 mins

Nutritional Information:

Calories	652 kcal
Carbohydrates	36.9 g
Cholesterol	111 mg
Fat	38.9 g
Fiber	2.9 g
Protein	37.1 g
Sodium	2696 mg

* Percent Daily Values are based on a 2,000 calorie diet.
☐

THE BEST PANINI DIP

Ingredients

- 1 tbsp mayonnaise
- 1 1/2 tsps hot pepper sauce
- 2 tsps garlic powder

Directions

- Combine all the ingredients very thoroughly in a bowl before refrigerating it for at least an hour.
- Serve with any Panini.

Serving: 1

Timing Information:

Preparation	Cooking	Total Time
5 mins		5 mins

Nutritional Information:

Calories	118 kcal
Carbohydrates	4.6 g
Cholesterol	5 mg
Fat	11 g
Fiber	0.6 g
Protein	1.1 g
Sodium	265 mg

* Percent Daily Values are based on a 2,000 calorie diet.

☐

YOGURT, PARMESAN, BASIL, TURKEY

Ingredients

- 3 tbsps reduced-fat mayonnaise
- 2 tbsps nonfat plain yogurt
- 2 tbsps shredded Parmesan cheese
- 2 tbsps chopped fresh basil
- 1 tsp lemon juice
- Freshly ground pepper to taste
- 8 slices whole-wheat bread
- 8 oz thinly sliced reduced-sodium deli turkey
- 8 tomato slices
- 2 tsps canola oil

Directions

- Heat up your Panini grill according to the instruction of the manufacturer.

- Spread a mixture of mayonnaise, lemon juice, yogurt, Parmesan, basil and pepper over each half of the bread before putting turkey and tomato slices over the lower half, and closing it up to make a sandwich.
- Put some butter on top and cook this Panini in the preheated grill for about 4 minutes or until the outside is golden brown.

Serving: 4

Timing Information:

Preparation	Cooking	Total Time
15 mins	10 mins	25 mins

Nutritional Information:

Calories	279 kcal
Carbohydrates	26.9 g
Cholesterol	31 mg
Fat	9.7 g
Fiber	4.4 g
Protein	22.1 g
Sodium	673 mg

* Percent Daily Values are based on a 2,000 calorie diet.

CHICKEN BREAST, ZUCCHINI, PEPPER

Ingredients

- 1/2 C. Tuscan Dressing
- 2 (4 oz) boneless skinless chicken breast halves
- 1 red pepper, cut into strips
- 1 small zucchini, cut lengthwise in half, then sliced crosswise
- 4 slices Italian bread
- 1/2 C. KRAFT Shredded Low-Moisture Part-Skim Mozzarella Cheese
- 2 tbsps chopped fresh basil

Directions

- Coat a mixture of vegetables and chicken with dressing before refrigerating it for at least thirty minutes.

- Heat up your Panini grill according to the instruction of the manufacturer.
- Cook chicken and vegetables over medium heat in a skillet for about 10 minutes or until tender.
- Now fill up the bread slices with chicken, vegetables, basil and cheese.
- Put some dressing on top of the bread and cook this Panini in the preheated grill for about five minutes or until the outside is golden brown.

Serving: 2

Timing Information:

Preparation	Cooking	Total Time
10 mins	35 mins	45 mins

Nutritional Information:

Calories	597 kcal
Carbohydrates	32.5 g
Cholesterol	98 mg
Fat	34.1 g
Fiber	3 g
Protein	36.3 g
Sodium	979 mg

* Percent Daily Values are based on a 2,000 calorie diet.
☐

DESSERT PANINI

Ingredients

- 1 tsp butter
- 1/2 C. crunchy peanut butter
- 8 slices firm bread
- 1/2 C. semi-sweet chocolate chips

Directions

- Heat up your Panini grill according to the instruction of the manufacturer.
- Spread peanut butter and then chocolate over the lower half of the bread before closing it up with the upper half.
- Put some butter on top and cook this Panini in the preheated grill for about 4 minutes or until the outside is golden brown.

Serving: 4

Timing Information:

Preparation	Cooking	Total Time
10 mins	15 mins	25 mins

Nutritional Information:

Calories	433 kcal
Carbohydrates	45.5 g
Cholesterol	3 mg
Fat	25.1 g
Fiber	5 g
Protein	12.5 g
Sodium	507 mg

* Percent Daily Values are based on a 2,000 calorie diet.

☐

MUSTARD, PEAR, MOZZARELLA

Ingredients

- 4 slices bread
- 1 tbsp mustard
- 6 slices ham
- 1 pear, peeled and thinly sliced
- 2 dashes ground black pepper
- 1 C. shredded mozzarella cheese
- 1 tbsp light margarine (such as I Can't Believe It's Not Butter - Light ®)

Directions

- Heat up your Panini grill according to the instruction of the manufacturer.
- Spread mustard, ham, pepper and mozzarella cheese over each half of the bread before closing it up to make a sandwich.

- Put some margarine on top of each bread and cook this Panini in the preheated grill for about 4 minutes or until the outside is golden brown.

Serving: 2

Timing Information:

Preparation	Cooking	Total Time
5 mins	6 mins	11 mins

Nutritional Information:

Calories	357 kcal
Carbohydrates	40.8 g
Cholesterol	36 mg
Fat	13.6 g
Fiber	4.3 g
Protein	18.3 g
Sodium	844 mg

* Percent Daily Values are based on a 2,000 calorie diet.
□

TURKEY PROVOLONE, CIABATTA

Ingredients

- 1 tbsp butter, or more if needed
- 2 slices ciabatta bread
- 6 slices deli-style sliced turkey breast
- 2 slices provolone cheese
- 3 sun-dried tomatoes packed in oil, drained and chopped
- 1/2 tsp Italian seasoning

Directions

- Heat up your Panini grill according to the instruction of the manufacturer.
- Spread butter over one lower side of bread and then put turkey, provolone cheese, Italian seasoning and sun dried tomatoes before closing it up to make a sandwich.

- Put some margarine on top of each bread and cook this Panini in the preheated grill for about 5 minutes or until the outside is golden brown.

Serving: 1

Timing Information:

Preparation	Cooking	Total Time
10 mins	5 mins	15 mins

Nutritional Information:

Calories	792 kcal
Carbohydrates	66.7 g
Cholesterol	138 mg
Fat	34.9 g
Fiber	3.9 g
Protein	53 g
Sodium	3267 mg

* Percent Daily Values are based on a 2,000 calorie diet.
☐

CHIPOTLE PEPPER, BACON, SPINACH

Ingredients

- 8 slices bacon
- 1 tbsp butter
- 2 cloves garlic, diced
- 1/2 red onion, thinly sliced
- 3 C. fresh spinach leaves
- 1/2 C. reduced-fat mayonnaise
- 2 chipotle peppers in adobo sauce, diced
- 1 tsp adobo sauce from chipotle peppers
- 8 (4 inch) pieces focaccia bread
- 4 slices provolone cheese
- 1/2 lb sliced deli turkey meat

Directions

- Heat up your Panini grill according to the instruction of the manufacturer.

- Cook bacon over medium heat until brown before draining it using a paper towel.
- Now cook onion and garlic in hot butter for about ten minutes before adding spinach and cooking it for another three minutes.
- Spread a mixture of mayonnaise, adobo sauce and diced chipotle peppers along with a slice of cheese over the upper half of the bread before putting turkey, a bacon and spinach mixture over the lower half and closing it up to make a sandwich.
- Cook this Panini in the preheated grill for about 5 minutes or until the outside is golden brown.

Serving: 6

Timing Information:

Preparation	Cooking	Total Time
20 mins	20 mins	40 mins

Nutritional Information:

Calories	699 kcal
Carbohydrates	65.1 g
Cholesterol	81 mg
Fat	33.2 g
Fiber	4.1 g
Protein	34.5 g
Sodium	2276 mg

* Percent Daily Values are based on a 2,000 calorie diet.

DIJON, ROAST BEEF, ROQUEFORT

Ingredients

- 3 tbsps unsalted butter
- 6 large shallots, sliced
- salt and black pepper to taste
- 2 French baguettes, halved lengthwise
- 2 tbsps Dijon mustard, or to taste
- 1 C. Roquefort cheese, crumbled
- 1 lb thinly sliced deli roast beef
- 1/2 C. cold heavy cream
- 1 1/2 tbsps finely shredded horseradish root
- 1 pinch salt and white pepper to taste

Directions

- Cook sliced shallots in hot butter for about ten minutes before adding salt and pepper.

- Heat up your Panini grill according to the instruction of the manufacturer.
- Spread Dijon mustard and Roquefort over the upper half of baguettes before putting roast beef and cooked shallots over the lower closing it up to make a sandwich.
- Cook this Panini in the preheated grill for about 4 minutes or until the outside is golden brown.
- Serve this with a mixture of horseradish, heavy cream, salt and pepper.

Serving: 6

Timing Information:

Preparation	Cooking	Total Time
10 mins	15 mins	25 mins

Nutritional Information:

Calories	652 kcal
Carbohydrates	77.3 g
Cholesterol	96 mg
Fat	23.3 g
Fiber	3.1 g
Protein	34.7 g
Sodium	2113 mg

* Percent Daily Values are based on a 2,000 calorie diet.

☐

SALAMI, HAM, MOZZARELLA, OLIVES

Ingredients

- 1/2 C. finely chopped drained marinated pickled vegetables
- 1/4 C. finely chopped stuffed green olives
- 1 1/2 C. shredded Mozzarella
- 6 (4 inch) Italian bread buns, split
- 2 1/2 oz sliced salami
- 4 1/4 oz sliced deli Black Forest ham
- 1 tbsp olive oil

Directions

- Heat up your Panini grill according to the instruction of the manufacturer.
- Spread cheese over the lower half of the bread before putting meat,

a mixture of vegetables and olives and the remaining cheese before closing it up to make a sandwich.

- Cook this Panini in the preheated grill for about seven minutes or until the outside is golden brown.

Serving: 6

Timing Information:

Preparation	Cooking	Total Time
13 mins	7 mins	20 mins

Nutritional Information:

Calories	366 kcal
Carbohydrates	36.5 g
Cholesterol	37 mg
Fat	16.5 g
Fiber	1.9 g
Protein	17.2 g
Sodium	1108 mg

* Percent Daily Values are based on a 2,000 calorie diet.

Parmesan, Mozzarella, Chicken Cutlet

Ingredients

- 1/4 C. flour
- 1 tsp garlic powder
- 1/2 tsp salt
- 1/4 tsp black pepper
- 1 egg, beaten
- 1 C. panko bread crumbs
- 1/4 C. Parmesan cheese
- 4 small chicken cutlets
- 2 tbsps olive oil
- 4 slices fresh mozzarella cheese
- 1/4 C. Parmesan cheese
- 8 thick slices artisanal-style bread
- 1 jar tomato sauce

Directions

- Put a mixture of flour, salt, garlic powder and pepper, eggs and mixture of panko bread crumbs and parmesan cheese in three separate bowls.

- Now coat chicken by dipping it in all the bowls and set it aside.
- Now fry this chicken in hot olive oil for about four minutes each side.
- Spread tomato sauce, slice of cheese and parmesan cheese over chicken placed on bread.
- Now grill this in the Panini grill for 5 minutes or until the cheese has melted.
- Serve.

Serving: 4

Timing Information:

Preparation	Cooking	Total Time
10 mins	15 mins	25 mins

Nutritional Information:

Calories	646 kcal
Carbohydrates	68.5 g
Cholesterol	125 mg
Fat	24.3 g
Fiber	12.7 g
Protein	42.6 g
Sodium	1792 mg

* Percent Daily Values are based on a 2,000 calorie diet.
☐

Spinach, Turkey Ciabatta

Ingredients

- 1/2 ripe avocado
- 1/4 cup mayonnaise
- 2 ciabatta rolls
- 1 tablespoon olive oil, divided
- 2 slices provolone cheese
- 1 cup whole fresh spinach leaves, divided
- 1/4 pound honey turkey
- 2 roasted red peppers, sliced into strips

Directions

- Heat up your Panini grill according to the instruction of the manufacturer.
- Mash mayonnaise and avocado together very thoroughly in a bowl.

- Now grill lower half of the bread brushed with olive oil for a few minutes before putting provolone cheese, turkey breast, spinach leaves, avocado mixture and roasted red pepper before closing it up to make a sandwich.
- Spread cheese over the lower half of the bread before putting meat, mixture of vegetables and olives and remaining cheese before closing it up to make a sandwich.
- Cook this Panini in the preheated grill for about seven minutes or until the outside is golden brown.

Serving: 6

Timing Information:

Preparation	Cooking	Total Time
17 mins	8 mins	25 mins

Nutritional Information:

Calories	723 kcal
Carbohydrates	42.1 g
Cholesterol	62 mg
Fat	51.3 g
Fiber	5.9 g
Protein	25.3 g
Sodium	1720 mg

* Percent Daily Values are based on a 2,000 calorie diet.

BALSAMIC, PARMESAN, MUSHROOM

Ingredients

- 2 red bell peppers
- 4 portobello mushroom caps
- 1 C. fat-free balsamic vinaigrette
- 4 (1/2 inch thick) slices eggplant, peeled
- 1 tsp garlic powder
- 1 tsp onion powder
- 2 tsps grated Parmesan cheese
- 8 slices focaccia bread
- 1/4 C. fat free ranch dressing
- 4 thin slices Swiss cheese
- 4 thin slices Asiago cheese

☐

Directions

- The distance of your broiler rack should be about 6 inches from the heat source before heating up.

- Place peppers on a baking sheet after cutting them in half and removing seeds, stems and ribs.
- Now cook this under the preheated broiler for about 10 minutes before letting it cool down for 20 minutes, while covered with a plastic wrap.
- Refrigerate for the whole night
- Coat Portobello mushroom caps with balsamic vinaigrette before refrigerating it too for the whole night.
- Coat eggplant slices with onion powder and garlic powder before heating up the grill.
- Now cook these eggplant slices and also Portobello mushrooms on the preheated grill for about four minutes each.
- Spread ranch dressing over a slice of focaccia before placing a slice of cheese, eggplant, roasted pepper and Portobello mushroom over bread very evenly.
- Close it up to form a sandwich.

- Now cook these sandwiches on the grill for about 5 minutes or until you see that it is golden brown in color.
- Serve.

Serving: 6

Timing Information:

Preparation	Cooking	Total Time
40 mins	20 mins	6 hr

Nutritional Information:

Calories	679 kcal
Carbohydrates	100.5 g
Cholesterol	46 mg
Fat	19 g
Fiber	10 g
Protein	28.1 g
Sodium	1779 mg

* Percent Daily Values are based on a 2,000 calorie diet.

A GIFT FROM ME TO YOU...

Send the Book!

I know you like easy cooking. But what about Japanese Sushi?

Join my private reader's club and get a copy of **_Infinite Sushi: A Complete Set of Sushi and Japanese Recipes_** by fellow BookSumo author Hashimoto Kazuma for FREE!

Send the Book!

Enjoy some of the best sushi available!

You will also receive updates about all my new books when they are free. So please show your support.

Also don't forget to like and subscribe on the social networks. I love meeting my readers. Links to all my profiles are below so please click and connect :)

Facebook

Twitter

COME ON...
LET'S BE FRIENDS :)

I adore my readers and love connecting with them socially. Please follow the links below so we can connect on Facebook, Twitter, and Google+.

Facebook

Twitter

I also have a blog that I regularly update for my readers so check it out below.

My Blog

Can I Ask A Favour?

If you found this book interesting, or have otherwise found any benefit in it. Then may I ask that you post a review of it on Amazon? Nothing excites me more than new reviews, especially reviews which suggest new topics for writing. I do read all reviews and I always factor feedback into my newer works.

So if you are willing to take ten minutes to write what you sincerely thought about this book then please visit our Amazon page and post your opinions.

Again thank you!

INTERESTED IN OTHER EASY COOKBOOKS?

Everything is easy! Check out my Amazon Author page for more great cookbooks:

For a complete listing of all my books please see my author page.

Made in the USA
San Bernardino, CA
13 December 2016